INTRODUCTION

Study skills are *learning skills*. One term is old, the other relatively new, but both have similar meanings. Study skills include a wide array of procedures which promote effective learning and good academic performance. These skills for learning also help students make good use of their time and resources.

STUDY SKILLS: WHAT ARE THEY?

Study skills are primarily information-processing procedures which facilitate the learning, retention, and application of knowledge and skill. Although some students may learn these procedures spontaneously or incidentally as a result of other instruction, most students learn study skills effectively only through direct, focused instruction.

Study skills, then, are learned abilities for acquiring and applying knowledge and skill. Learning study skills involves *learning how to learn.*

TRANSITION FROM HIGH SCHOOL TO COLLEGE

When students enter college, the most striking differences they find from high school are a considerably larger workload and a much greater need to learn effectively on their own. Some students respond well to these challenges, with greater or lesser struggles, and go on to success. Others adjust only to some extent and are hampered throughout their college careers. Still others fail to cope satisfactorily and leave school.

The central value underlying the *hm College Study Skills Program* is that we have a responsibility and an opportunity to help students prepare for college work. The more we can aid them in their development of a repertoire of useful study skills which are appropriate for college level work, the more prepared they will be and, thus, the more successful they will be in college. When students develop a repertoire of study skills, they become both more *independent* as learners and more *efficient* in their learning.

Mastering and using study skills give students a sense of empowerment, of being capable. And that experience of capability breeds a sense of confidence in their own ability to learn, understand, and succeed. When we engage students towards the end of high school or during their first semester in college in the learning and use of college study skills, we can contribute to their potential for empowerment and success as learners both in college and throughout their lives.

THE hm COLLEGE STUDY SKILLS PROGRAM

The *hm College Study Skills Program* is designed to provide *an introduction to the study skills needed for college work* for students in grades 11–13.

The *hm Program* includes 12 activity-oriented units and an Introduction which is itself an activity. Most of the units require from 70–100 minutes of instructional time.

The *hm Program* is structured on the assumption that activity-oriented lessons are a most effective way to teach study skills; more succinctly, that "learning by doing" is the best way to master skills. The program is also based on the values below:

1. Study skills are skills for learning, information-processing procedures which facilitate the learning, retention, and application of knowledge and skill.
2. Study skills are as basic and important as any skills which we can teach in schools.
3. Learning by doing is the only effective way to learn study skills.
4. An important aspect of learning study skills involves learning more about how one learns, that is, one's learning style. Instruction in study skills engages the student in an active participation in her or his own learning. The student is encouraged and provided with the opportunity to develop the ability to exercise his or her own judgment in relation to learning.
5. A considerable part of study skills instruction ought to take place in structured school settings. Whenever possible, study skills instruction should be integrated with the regular curriculum of a class or course. (When this is not possible, study skills teaching and learning should at least be tied to the student's regular course work.)
6. The learning of study skills offers the potential for a transfer effect: a study skill learned in one context may be used in many others.
7. The work of various developmental psychologists, particularly Piaget, has shown us that there is a continuum of cognitive development throughout the years of childhood and adolescence. It is crucial to relate these insights to the teaching of study skills and to ask a student to learn only what is within the realm of her or his developmental level.

college study skills program Level III

INTRODUCTION AND SAMPLE UNIT

AMERICAN COUNCIL ON EDUCATION

nassp

The *hm Program* is deliberately designed to address a wide range of student needs, allow for the participation of students with a diversity of skills, and promote learning on various levels of competence.

The *hm Program* includes the following units:

Introduction To Study Skills And Learning Style

I. Listening Is Tuning In
II. Taking Notes Is A College Survival Skill
III. Learning To Survey
IV. Thinking About New Words
V. Asking Useful Questions
VI. Learning From Your Reading
VII. Taking Charge Of Your Learning
VIII. Understanding And Improving Your Memory
IX. Reading Flexibly
X. Gaining From Discussions
XI. Learning From Visuals
XII. Preparing For And Taking Exams

USING THE hm COLLEGE STUDY SKILLS PROGRAM: WHERE AND WHEN

Our classroom testing has shown that the *hm College Study Skills Program* is effective and valuable both at the high school and college levels.

In high school, the *hm Program* can be integrated into an existing 12th grade course or group of courses. (Some schools have also used the *Program* with 11th graders of high ability.) We suggest that you may want to teach the *Study Skills Program* during the second semester of the senior year when students know they are college bound and have already turned their attention in that direction.

If you choose not to integrate the *hm Program* into an existing course, it can still be used, although we believe it will be less effective. If you use the *hm Program* in a separate setting, be sure to have students work with their assignments from their regular courses in the context of their learning about study skills.

In college, the *hm Study Skills Program* can be integrated into an existing course. Or, the *hm Program* may be taught in a "learning skills" or "learning assistance" setting. If you use the *Program* in this way, be sure to have students bring their actual course work into your class and begin to apply the study skills they learn from the *hm Program* to that work.

In college or high school, learning new skills requires time and practice. People learn skills through processes of repeated trial and error. We try a new skill, make mistakes, identify and learn from our mistakes, and then correct them. The *hm College Study Skills Program* provides only one practice for each skill which it introduces. If your students are to master the various study skills presented here, it is essential that you provide them with and/or guide them to opportunities for practice of the study skills.

Given this need for trial and error practice, we suggest that you introduce at most only one unit each week.

SUGGESTIONS FOR TEACHING THE hm COLLEGE STUDY SKILLS PROGRAM

The *hm College Study Skills Program* is designed to be taught by an instructor working with a group of students. The *Program* can be used effectively with classes or groups as small as five or six.

Suggested Directions

The Instructor's Guide offers "Suggested Directions" for teaching each unit in the *Program.* Our classroom testing has shown these methods to be useful. Of course, we invite you to adapt them in ways which you see fit.

We suggest that you examine both the Student Text and the Instructor's Guide carefully prior to your teaching of the various units.

Suggested Times

Each section within the "Suggested Directions" includes approximate times for the activities in that section. Most of the units range from 70–100 minutes. To save class time, you may want to assign sections of some units for homework.

We caution you that these times are approximate. Our classroom testing has shown us that the wide variation in teaching styles results in an equally wide range in the pacing of instruction. We strongly suggest that you examine the units carefully and gauge your planning of instructional time according to your knowledge of how things work in your classroom.

Introduction To The Student Text

Note that the "Introduction To Study Skills" in the student text is an activity-oriented unit in itself. It introduces students to the concepts of study skills and learning style and the relationship between them.

This "Introduction" is actually the first unit in the book and should be taught as any other unit.

Unit Summaries

Each unit includes a summary at the end. While the use of these summaries has not been formally integrated into the "Suggested Directions" for instruction, we recommend that you bring the summaries to the attention of your students.

You will also find each summary included with its unit in the Instructor's Guide.

Learning Study Skills On Your Own

At the end of each unit, students will find a brief section entitled "Learning Study Skills On Your Own." These resources are designed to give students an opportunity to explore their own learning and study skills independently. Each section gives an introduction to a skill or concept and directions through which to pursue it.

You may want to call your students' attention to these resources.

Extension Activities

Each unit includes a list of "Extension Activities" which provide you with many ideas for further instruction in all of the study skill areas included in the *hm Program.*

TEACHING THE hm COLLEGE STUDY SKILLS PROGRAM: IMPORTANT ISSUES

Learning Style

An awareness of and sensitivity to individual learning style differences is one of the central values in the *hm College Study Skills Program.* Students are introduced to the concept of learning style and work with it in a variety of ways throughout the *Program.*

If you are not familiar with recent work in the learning style field, we suggest that you examine *Student Learning Styles: Diagnosing and Prescribing Programs* (Reston, Virginia: National Association of Secondary School Principals, 1979) as a first step in your own education about learning style. Once you've read this collection of articles, you will have many directions which you can then pursue.

Small Groups

For many of the activities in the *hm Program,* we suggest that students work in pairs or small groups. The interaction of students working on a common task can facilitate the learning of skills through shared problem solving.

Small group processes offer a superb method for genuinely engaging students in an activity. Such processes help both to enhance motivation for learning and to increase interest in the content of the lesson, as they offer active participation to each and every student.

Small groups also provide students with a forum where they can discuss their learning with a minimum of risk.

Individual Work in Study Skills

Individual work is of critical importance to the learning of skills. When a study skill is introduced in a group setting, it becomes crucial to provide individual work with that skill through homework and/or other class activities.

Student Perceptions and Expectations

Sometimes students perceive new study skills as more time consuming than their unskilled learning behaviors. In a few cases, this is an accurate perception, but most often it is not.

You can help students gain a wider perspective about their own learning by telling them that any skill, by its very nature, takes more time to use when you are first learning how to do it. Then, as you become more competent in using the skill, it takes less and less time. Ask students to think of examples of this from their own experience. Or, give them a few examples which will illustrate this relationship between competence and time.

Grading

If you teach in an environment where students will only attend seriously to that which is graded, that is, to that which "counts," then we suggest that you grade study skills work in some fair and concrete manner. Your standard of evaluation ought to keep in mind how study skills are learned, namely through repeated practice over time, and set reasonable levels of expected mastery.

If you do not need to grade students' work to encourage their serious participation in the units of the *hm Program,* then we see no reason to do so.

OTHER hm STUDY SKILLS PROGRAMS

The **hm Study Skills Program** includes the following:

The **hm Study Skills Program Level B** .... for grades 3–4
The **hm Study Skills Program Level I** .... for grades 5–7
The **hm Study Skills Program Level II** .... for grades 8–10
The **hm Study Skills Program Level III** .... for grades 11–13
The **hm Math Study Skills Program** .... for grades 6–10
The **hm Science Study Skills Program** .... for grades 7–10
The **hm GED Study Skills Program** .... for Adults

UNIT IX: READING FLEXIBLY

Many research studies have demonstrated that one of the most important characteristics of excellent readers is their ability to change their reading rate depending on (1) the kind of material being read; (2) the purpose for reading; and (3) the difficulty of reading material in terms of their own background. The ability to change reading rate in light of these factors is called *reading flexibility*.

Poor and average readers tend to read everything from "Dear Abby" to a physics text at the same rate. They begin with the title and plod through every word until they reach the end. In contrast, excellent readers quickly survey their task first and choose an appropriate rate of reading. Depending on the material and their purpose, they may read only for main ideas and skim over or omit examples, details, and even whole sections if they find them irrelevant to their goals. Or, they may read slowly with painstaking care.

The purpose of this unit is to introduce students to the idea of reading flexibly, that is, changing their reading rate to meet their needs. The unit is also designed to involve students in some initial practice of the skills involved in flexible reading.

Please Note: For *Practice 4* on page 85, students will need to use one of their own textbooks. Be sure to ask them to bring a textbook to class on the day when you work on this practice.

READING FLEXIBILITY — CHANGE AND GUILT

Some students may ask: "Why shouldn't I read slowly and carefully? I've always done my reading that way, and my grades are good."

You may want to respond to this by noting that many students do well, particularly in high school, in spite of their slow reading rate, not because of it. You may also want to sketch out the much heavier reading load which students face in college compared to that in high school.

Another kind of response involves stressing the ways in which flexible reading is more efficient than one slow reading rate. Some of these are:

1. Flexible reading is more efficient. You can accomplish more in the same amount of time.
2. Flexible reading aids comprehension. Slow readers do not comprehend as well as readers of similar ability who vary their rate. Slow readers can't interrelate information as well as flexible readers.
3. Flexible reading is directed. You focus your effort on what's important.
4. Flexible reading aids memory. When you think about what's important in a reading and set a framework for it, you're much more likely to retain it.
5. Flexible reading is the most feasible way to complete college reading assignments successfully.

It's natural for students to feel committed to habits which they believe helped them to succeed in the past. The most respectful and effective way to teach flexible reading is to explain what the skills are and why they work, give students an opportunity to try them, and help students discover the benefits of flexible reading through their analysis of their own experience.

A final word: some students feel guilty if they don't read every word in an assignment. You may want to address this concern by discussing it in terms of the student's purpose for reading. Focus on the idea that you read for a purpose. Often you don't need to read every word, every section, or even every assignment to achieve your purpose. And there's nothing wrong with omitting that which you know you don't need. You might also want to share some of your own experience of learning to become a flexible reader.

FLEXIBLE READING AND SPEED READING

Flexible reading is *not* speed reading, although speed reading may be one rate which a reader uses. It's important to note that this unit does not teach speed reading.

The value of speed reading is discussed in the "Learning Study Skills On Your Own" section at the end of the unit. Speed reading is a relatively simple and immensely valuable skill which, for some reason, schools have almost totally ignored. We urge you to examine this skill carefully in the source cited in "Learning Study Skills On Your Own" and elsewhere. You may want to develop your own speed reading skills and then help your students develop theirs.

USING AN ENCYCLOPEDIA

Although some college instructors will not permit the use of an encyclopedia as a source, an encyclopedia entry is still a good starting point for a student who is tackling an unfamiliar subject. In view of this value (and aware of possible protests), we have included an entry from an encyclopedia as a resource in this unit.

Suggested Directions for Unit IX

1. Have your students read "What Is Flexible Reading?" (page 82). Discuss the three factors which affect rate. Have several students share their own examples for each factor.

   Approximate time: 3-5 minutes

2. Have your students complete Practice 1 (page 82). Tell them that they will come back to it in a few minutes. Then, ask them to read "Different Rates Of Reading" (pages 82-83). Discuss each of the four rates. Have students give examples of when they use each.

   Approximate time: 7 minutes

3. Have your students do Practice 2 (page 83). Discuss the ways in which reading rates do (or should) vary for different kinds of reading. Ask students to give examples from their responses to Practices 1 and 2.

   Approximate time: 5 minutes

4. Ask your students to read "Using Different Reading Rates" (page 83) and do Practice 3 (pages 83-84). When they are done, have them form pairs, and ask them to share their questions, answers, and other notes with each other. Then, discuss the different rates of reading they used with the whole class.

   Approximate time: 15-20 minutes

5. Have your students read "Using Your Rapid Reading Rate" (page 85) and the directions for Practice 4 (page 85). Discuss as is useful. Tell students that you will announce the timing. (Some students may complain about the brevity of time allowed. Encourage them just to try it out and see what happens.) Give them 3 minutes to survey, then 8 minutes to read rapidly. Ask your students to discuss their experience with their partners for a few minutes. Then, engage them in a whole class discussion about the usefulness of rapid reading. Ask several students to share their estimations.

   Approximate time: 20 minutes

6. Give students the choice of working on the rest of the unit individually or in pairs. When they have decided, have them read "Flexible Reading For Research" (page 85). Discuss as is needed. Then, ask students to do Practice 5 (pages 85-86) and Practice 6 (page 86). When they are done, go over the practices.

   Approximate time: 10-15 minutes

7. Have your students do Practice 7 (pages 86-88). Go over their responses to the questions and the various sections of the article which they marked. (You may want to do this with the whole class or in small groups.) Then, have students discuss their experience of reading flexibly.

   Approximate time: 20 minutes

8. Follow the same procedure for Practice 8 (pages 88-89) as you did for Practice 7.

   Approximate time: 15-20 minutes

ANSWERS FOR PRACTICES IN UNIT IX

Pages 82-83: Practices 1-2

Answers will vary.

Pages 83-84: Practice 3

Questions, answers, and notes will vary. Questions should include some of the following:

What is the "third world"?	"Have-not" countries, mostly undeveloped, whose interests are different from the "free" and Communist "worlds."
Does the "third world" have clout in global affairs?	Yes, based on control of natural resources and large numbers in the UN General Assembly and other bodies.
Are all "third world" nations poor?	No. Another determination of inclusion is a feeling of having been cheated by lighter-skinned, "northern" nations. Most of the "third world" countries are "southern," have darker-skinned populations.

Who are the targets of the "third world"?	USA, Western European nations, Soviet Union.
Does the talk of different worlds really mean something?	Yes. It has both moral and economic aspects to it, and it's very real.

Page 86: Practice 5

Arlex, Bertrand, Jackson, Richards

Check "Richards" twice as it is directly relevant and most current.

Page 86: Practice 6

Applications: medicine	Dental drilling
Applied laser principles	Fiber-optic scalpel
Bloodless surgery	Surgery

If students can support other answers than those above, accept them.

Pages 86–88: Practice 7

Answers will vary. Accept any answers which students can support. Suggested answers are as follows:

Checks next to: paragraphs 1, 2, 3 and possibly 4 in the first section
the paragraph "In Medicine"
paragraphs 1–4 in "How a Laser Works"

X next to: will vary; ask students to explain their choices

1. The rest of the article would not be helpful, unless the student wants to include material about the history of lasers in the paper's introduction.
2. Answers will vary. Ask students to explain their choices.

Pages 88–89: Practice 8

Answers will vary. Accept any answers which students can support. Suggested answers are:

Checks next to: paragraphs in the "Medicine" section

1–3. Answers will vary.

EXTENSION ACTIVITIES

1. Have students establish their "four" reading rates. Time them on materials that call for all four rates. Be sure to check comprehension in some way. Encourage students to practice the four rates for two or three weeks, and time them again for comparison.

   You may want to have students record their results on a chart like the one below.

STUDENT DIRECTIONS AND CHART:

For a few weeks, fill in the chart to analyze your reading flexibility. Beside each rate note the book or magazine you use. (Don't use more than one book or magazine for each rate, or you won't be comparing similar things.) Write the amount of time you practice each rate each day or so. Then, write the number of pages read (use fractions if necessary) and under it a "+" for good comprehension or a "−" for poor comprehension.

RATES	BOOK OR JOURNAL	TIME	PAGES READ/COMPREHENSION
SKIM			
RAPID			
AVERAGE			
SLOW			

2. Encourage students to read chapters of a textbook or other non-fiction book as they did in Practice 4. Ask them to aim at completing the survey/rapid reading of a chapter in 30 minutes or less. Later they can read in more detail and take notes, if necessary.

3. Teach the *paper clip technique.* Have students read a fairly easy book for 10 minutes and mark where they end. Next, they count the pages they read. Then, they take a paperclip and attach it one page beyond the number of pages they just read. Allow 10 minutes to reach the clip. Each time they read, have them add one or one-half page to be read in the same amount of time.

   Be sure to allow recall time after each reading.

UNIT IX SUMMARY: READING FLEXIBLY

Flexible reading means learning to vary your reading rate according to:

1. The kind of material you are reading
2. The purpose for which you are reading
3. The difficulty of the reading material for you

Think of flexible reading as shifting into different gears depending on what you are reading and for what purpose.

Four different reading rates are:

1. Skimming and scanning rate	Reading only key words, phrases, and sentences. Or, quickly searching for particular information. A very fast rate useful for surveying and finding specific information.
2. Rapid reading rate	Pushing your normal reading rate faster on purpose. Useful when you are reading only for main ideas or for review.
3. Average reading rate	The rate at which you ordinarily read material of average difficulty. Useful when you want to know details as well as main ideas.
4. Slow reading rate	Reading more slowly and deliberately than your average reading rate. Useful for difficult and/or technical reading.

For actual reading, you'll want to use several or all four rates while you read a chapter or article. The skilled reader changes gears often.

Reading flexibly can help you do research for research papers more effectively and efficiently. For example, you can skim or scan the entries in a card catalogue to find ones which are relevant for your topic. Once you locate useful books, you can skim their indexes to help you locate passages in the books which are directly related to your topic.

When you read any sources, for example, journal articles or articles in encyclopedias or elsewhere, you can use skimming, rapid reading, average reading, and slow reading as these rates are helpful to you.

UNIT IX: READING FLEXIBLY

WHAT IS FLEXIBLE READING?

Many people read everything from the most entertaining mystery to the most densely written science text at exactly the same rate. They don't read flexibly at all. Despite vast differences in how difficult the reading material is and for what purpose they are reading, many people don't know how to vary their reading speed.

One of the most valuable and time-saving study skills is *flexible reading.* This skill means learning to vary your reading rate according to:

1. The *kind of material* you are reading; for example, an article from a science magazine is usually more packed with new ideas and vocabulary and, therefore, more difficult than most short stories.
2. The *purpose* for which you are reading; for example, finding one particular piece of information in a chapter can be accomplished with a much quicker reading speed than finding all the main ideas and important details in that chapter.
3. The *difficulty* of the material *for you:* for example, if you know a lot about music but don't know much about sports, you can probably read an article about music more quickly than one about sports.

Think of flexible reading as shifting into different gears depending on what you are reading and for what purpose.

Practice 1: On the lines below, list the kinds of material you read in a typical month, i.e., newspaper, telephone book, signs, history text, etc. Don't write anything inside the parentheses yet.

______________________	( )	______________________	( )
______________________	( )	______________________	( )
______________________	( )	______________________	( )
______________________	( )	______________________	( )
______________________	( )	______________________	( )

DIFFERENT RATES OF READING

Below you'll find descriptions of four different reading rates:

1. **SKIMMING AND SCANNING RATE**

   Skimming means reading only key words, phrases, and sentences in a piece of text. It is a very fast rate through which you can gain a general sense of what the text is about, for example, in a survey. *Scanning* means quickly searching a piece of text for some particular information. It is usually an even faster rate than skimming and is used, for example, to locate information in an index.

2. **RAPID READING RATE**

   At this rate you are deliberately reading faster than you normally read. You are consciously trying to read quickly. This rate is appropriate when you read newspapers and magazines, when you are reading only for main ideas, and when you are reading for review.

3. **AVERAGE READING RATE**

This is the rate at which you ordinarily read. Use it for material of average difficulty which you want to recall later, for example, books with literary value, articles for assignments, and selections in which you want to know details as well as main ideas. You'll often want to use this rate for textbooks which are not technical.

4. **SLOW READING RATE**

This rate is slower and more deliberate than your average rate. Use it when the material is difficult and demands that you pay more attention to each word, for example, with technical articles or texts. Or, use it when you want to take detailed notes from your reading.

In actual reading, you'll find that your use of these different rates will certainly overlap. You will want to use several rates and perhaps all four while you read one chapter or article. The skilled reader changes gears often.

Practice 2: In the parentheses next to each type of reading you listed in Practice 1, write the number(s) of the reading rate(s) you would use for that type of reading. Be able to explain your choices.

1 = skimming and scanning rate

2 = rapid reading rate

3 = average reading rate

4 = slow reading rate

USING DIFFERENT READING RATES

In this unit, you'll practice ways of applying different reading rates to several practical reading and study situations.

One way that you already know to use different reading rates is the surveying/questioning/reading method. First you survey an article at a skimming rate, keying on important questions. Then you read at an average rate, or faster or slower as the material demands, to answer your questions.

You've already used this survey/question/read method in other units. When you try it again in Practice 3, be aware of your changing reading rate.

Practice 3: Survey the article on page 84, using your skimming rate. In the spaces below, write three questions you can use to help guide your more careful reading of the article.

QUESTIONS

1. ______________________________

2. ______________________________

3. ______________________________

Now, read the article at your average rate, or slower or faster as the material requires. Answer your questions on the lines below (unless you find a question is not worth answering). If you find important information not covered by your questions, note it on the lines at the top of the next page.

ANSWERS

1. ______________________________

____

2. ______________________________

____

3. ______________________________

____

OTHER NOTES

We've Been Asked

WHAT IS THE "THIRD WORLD"?

From Top Authorities Come Answers to Questions on Topics in the News

We hear more and more about the "third world." What is it?

First off, it's not an organization in any formal sense. It doesn't even have a membership roll.

In general, what is regarded as the "third world" consists of "have not" nations, still undeveloped, whose interests don't jibe with those of developed nations in the other two "worlds" — that is, the Communist and non-Communist "worlds."

But isn't it generally credited with having a great deal of clout in global affairs? How can that be?

The "third world" has been wielding unexpected strength, partly because of sheer numbers — and partly for other reasons.

For example, look at the oil-producing countries, most of them generally listed as "third world." They are in a cartel, and their ability to impose higher oil prices on richer nations — or even reduce the flow of petroleum — has been amply demonstrated. That's real clout in a global economy so dependent on oil.

And some other "third world" nations are trying to get in on the act. They are now organizing cartels in an effort to control supply and prices of their exports — principally bauxite, copper, sugar and coffee.

Getting back to the power of numbers: The United Nations General Assembly has more and more been turned into a forum for the "third world." It now wields a majority there.

During the last session of the Assembly, a Mexican-sponsored "economic charter" — which included approval of expropriation of foreign-owned property subject only to domestic laws — was passed by 115 votes to 6, with 10 abstentions. It had solid "third world" backing.

Isn't there a tighter definition of the "third world"? After all, Saudi Arabia isn't exactly poor.

Poverty isn't the only factor. A nation is likely to consider itself on the "outside" — and thus part of the "third world" — when its people have a highly emotional conviction that, throughout history, they've been cheated by richer nations.

These people sometimes want more than just a more-equitable distribution of the world's wealth. They may want revenge for wrongs of the past.

Another way to put it: The "third world" in general is the southern poorer half of the Earth pitted against the richer northern half. You might even detect a racial connection — the darker-skinned peoples getting together to demand "economic justice" from the lighter-skinned populations.

Who are the specific targets of the "third world" revolt?

The U.S., the richest country, is always the chief target. Next in priority are Western Europe and Japan.

The Soviet Union lays claim to strong links with the "third world" because it is "socialist," anti-capitalist and anti-imperialist. Yet most of the "third world" nations consider Russia just another "have" superpower.

Mainland China insists it will never become a superpower and claims to be on the side of "oppressed" peoples." Where does it fit in?

At the U.N., "third world" nations welcome Peking's support — but are wary of China's potential power.

How did the three-world concept come about? Isn't the world supposed to be getting smaller?

Certainly, satellite communication and jet travel have in a sense been shrinking the world. But that's part of the whole problem. Now you find peoples of the "have not" nations far more aware of just how little they actually have, compared with the two other "worlds." Once they were fairly ignorant of that fact.

Today they are far more sophisticated about economics and sharing the wealth. You find the full thrust for redistribution of the world's riches centered on the poor of the "third world" rallying together against the wealthy of the "first" and "second" worlds led by the U.S. and Russia.

So to judge who's in the "third world," it's more than just a question of examining a nation's budget or trade balance.

It certainly is — and even experts have trouble fitting countries into slots.

A good way to start, though, is to separate out those countries which belong to regional alliances such as NATO and the Warsaw Pact. The remaining countries are eligible to call themselves "nonaligned."

Then you have to consider whether the people of a country are poor — and if they feel they have been abused economically or politically over long periods by "colonial" or "imperialist" powers.

Does all this talk of different "worlds" really mean anything?

Very much so. Citizens of wealthy countries, especially Americans, are being inundated with demands by people from the poorer nations for a better life.

Leaders of all walks of life in the U.S. say this is a moral challenge that cannot be ignored.

On the dollars-and-cents level, the new-found unity among the "third world" nations can mean America will have to pay a lot more for the raw materials that support its high standard of living.

Nevertheless, the world is changing fast, and so is U.S. policy. American experts hope that an acceptable adjustment — for both moral and economic reasons — can be worked out between the "have" countries and the "have nots" of the "third world."

USING YOUR RAPID READING RATE

In certain situations, you can use your rapid reading rate to help you become more efficient in your reading. When your time for reading is limited, when you only want or need to gain a general idea of what the reading is about, or when you want to get a sense of a topic before a lecture, use your rapid reading rate as follows:

1. First, survey the article, chapter, or book quickly. Use your survey to "size up" the reading. Decide which parts or sections are useful or interesting to you. (Sometimes a survey may help you decide not to read the material at all.)
2. Next, use your rapid reading rate to read the important sections of the chapter, article, or book. As you read, focus your attention on the main ideas. Don't worry about details. If you need them, you can always return to find them. And don't feel guilty about not reading every word. An efficient reader picks and chooses what she or he reads.
3. Take a minute and review the main ideas in the reading.

Practice 4: Select a chapter which you haven't read in the textbook you've brought to class. Take *3 minutes* to survey the chapter. Then, use your rapid reading rate to read as much as you can of the important sections in that chapter in *8 minutes.* You may not finish, but see how far you get.

When you stop, estimate how long it would have taken you to read all of the important sections in the chapter at your rapid reading rate. Write your estimate in the space below.

_______ minutes

Now, estimate how long it would take you to review the main ideas you've read so far in this chapter. Write your estimate in the space below.

_______ minutes

FLEXIBLE READING FOR RESEARCH

Many college courses require you to do research and write a research paper. For this task flexible reading will prove extremely valuable. You'll be shifting your reading gears again and again as you work through the various steps in writing a research paper.

For the rest of the practices in this unit, imagine that you've been assigned a research paper in your introductory Science and Society course. Although you don't know much about them, you are interested in *lasers.* So you've chosen that as your topic. The paper assignment asks you to choose a recent scientific development and investigate both what it is and one way in which people use it. You know that lasers have medical uses, so you narrow your topic to *the medical uses of lasers.* (Later you might want to narrow the topic further.)

In these practices, first you'll skim as you look for books in the *card catalogue* and for references to your subject in the *index* of a book about lasers. You'll use several rates to read and take notes from an *encyclopedia article* and from a *journal article.*

Practice 5: One use of your fastest reading rate is skimming the library card catalogue or a bibliography to find the best sources for your paper. Once you find your subject in the card catalogue or in a bibliography, you can skim all of the included entries to find the ones most likely to be helpful to you.

Skim the card catalogue entries on the next page. Place a checkmark on the line before any item which you think might be a good source for a paper about "The Medical Uses of Lasers." (For most research papers, you'll want to choose the most up-to-date sources.) When you are done, place a second check next to the item which you think will be your *best* source.

____ Allen, Benjamin. *Lasers for Communication.* Chicago: The Tower Press, 1979.

____ Arlex, Susan T. "Is Laser Surgery Safe?" *Modern Health,* XIV (June 10, 1978), pp. 85-87.

____ Bertrand, James. "Advantages of Lasers in Opthalmology." *Science for Today.* VII (July 17, 1981), pp. 67-71.

____ Collins, Richard. *Circuitry for Semiconductor Lasers.* Chicago: Scientific Press, 1982.

____ Howard, Nancy P. "How Laser Accidents Occur in the Laboratory." *American Times,* XII (1980), 17-22.

____ Jackson, Donald. *Laser Applications.* Milwaukee: University Press, 1980.

____ King, Anne P. "Lasers Used in Engineering." *Engineering Weekly,* X (March 2, 1979), pp. 12-15.

____ Richards, Mary. *Medical Uses of Lasers.* New York: Medical Publishing Company, 1982.

Practice 6: Imagine that you've located an appropriate book about lasers in the library. You'll want to turn to the book's index and skim the entries to find the information you seek.

You know that you want information about *the medical uses of lasers.* You also need some general information about *how lasers work* for the first part of your paper.

Skim the sample index entries below to find information about (1) how lasers work, and (2) the medical uses of lasers. Place a check on the line before each entry which you think will be useful to you.

INDEX FOR BOOK ON LASERS

Applications,

____ Communications, 35-40
____ Engineering, 41-50
____ Holography, 51-53
____ Medicine, 54-62

____ Applied laser principles, 3-25

____ Bloodless surgery, 55

____ Building construction, 41-45

____ Dental drilling, 61-62

____ Energy, 27-30

____ Fiber-optic scalpel, 56

____ Fire alarm system, 50

Light,

____ Fibers, 97-99
____ Waves, 15-17

____ Radio waves, 100-105

____ Surgery, 54-60

Practice 7: You might choose to read an encyclopedia article about lasers to give you some background on the topic. On pages 87-88, you'll find such an article.

Read the article *flexibly.* Place a check in the margin next to any paragraph which relates to your paper topic.

Place an X next to any paragraph which you will skip entirely.

When you have finished reading, answer the two questions on page 88.

Remember: you're interested in how lasers work and what their medical uses are.

LASER is a device that *amplifies* (strengthens) light. A laser produces a thin beam of light that can burn a hole in a diamond or carry the signals of many different television pictures at the same time. The word *laser* stands for **l**ight **a**mplification by **s**timulated **e**mission of **r**adiation.

The light from a laser differs from the light produced by other sources, such as electric bulbs, fluorescent lamps, and the sun. The light from these other sources travels in all directions. The light from a laser is highly directional. In other words, it travels in only one direction. It travels in a narrow beam, and the sides of the beam stay almost parallel. For example, a beam ½ inch (13 millimeters) wide may spread to only about 3 inches (7.6 centimeters) after traveling a distance of a mile (1.6 kilometers).

Laser light also differs from other light in terms of *frequency,* the number of vibrations of a light wave per second. The light from a laser consists of one or, at most, a few frequencies. The light from other sources consists of many frequencies. Because laser light has so few frequencies, a laser beam has a narrow frequency range on the *electromagnetic spectrum,* an arrangement of frequencies from lowest to highest.

The frequencies of a laser beam may be in only the visible region of the electromagnetic spectrum. Or they may be in only the infrared or ultraviolet regions, both of which are invisible. The frequencies of light produced by most other sources are in the visible and invisible regions of the electromagnetic spectrum at the same time. See ELECTROMAGNETIC WAVES (The Electromagnetic Spectrum).

How Lasers Are Used

The unusual characteristics of laser light make lasers a valuable tool in (1) communications, (2) industry, (3) medicine, (4) military operations, and (5) scientific research.

In Communications, a laser can transmit voice messages and television signals. It has great advantages over ordinary electronic transmitters, such as those used to produce radio and television signals. For example, a laser operates at a much higher frequency than do electronic transmitters. The high frequency of laser light enables a laser beam to carry much more information than radio waves can. Therefore, one of these beams can transmit many telephone calls and television programs at the same time.

A laser can transmit information with little interference because it produces a highly directional beam. A laser beam can be directed to fall solely on the desired laser-receiving equipment. Because the equipment receives only the laser beam directed at it, most interference is eliminated.

A laser also may serve as an efficient long-distance transmitter because of its highly directional beam. Laser beams, unlike radio waves, spread only slightly as they travel. For this reason, scientists believe a laser beam may provide an excellent communications link with spacecraft. On the earth, a laser beam may be sent from one relay station to another through a long glass fiber. The beam is reflected through the fiber and can travel great distances with little loss of energy (see FIBER OPTICS).

In Industry, the laser has a variety of uses. For example, it may be used as a source of intense heat. The sides of a laser beam are nearly parallel, and so a lens can focus the beam to a point only 1/10,000 inch (0.0025 millimeter) wide. When the beam is concentrated on such a small area, it may produce temperatures higher than 10,000°F. (5538°C). In this way, a laser beam can be used to melt extremely hard materials.

Manufacturers use short bursts of laser light to weld miniature metal parts together in electronic equipment. For example, a laser can be used to connect wires sealed inside a glass tube. In heavy industry, high-power lasers are used to weld large metal parts together. Surveyors use a laser range finder to measure distances in making maps.

In Medicine, surgeons use the heating action of a laser beam to remove diseased body tissue. The beam burns away the unhealthy tissue in a fraction of a second with little damage to the surrounding healthy area. Eye specialists use the laser to correct a condition called *retinal detachment* (see EYE [Diseases]). They aim a laser beam into the patient's eye and focus it on the retina. The heat of the beam "welds" the loose retina into place.

In Military Operations, a laser beam can be bounced off a target, such as an enemy airplane or ship, to determine its distance and speed. Laser *gyroscopes* (guidance devices) are being developed to direct bombs and artillery shells to their target. Laser range finders and gyroscopes may be used in commercial navigation as well as by military forces.

In Scientific Research, a laser has many uses. For example, it may be used to create hot gases called *plasmas.* The study of plasmas may help scientists learn to control *nuclear fusion,* the process by which lightweight atoms combine into heavier ones to produce energy. The control of this process and the use of lasers in similar research could help solve the energy needs of mankind. See NUCLEAR ENERGY (Nuclear Fusion).

How a Laser Works

Light is a form of energy that is released from individual atoms or molecules in a substance. To understand how a laser works, it is necessary to know something about the nature of atoms and how they interact with light and other forms of energy.

Every atom is a storehouse of energy. The amount of energy in an atom depends on the motion of the electrons that orbit the atom's nucleus. When an atom absorbs energy, its energy level increases, and the atom is said to be *excited.* The atoms of a substance become excited when they absorb heat, light, or other forms of energy that pass through the substance. An excited atom can return to its normal energy level by releasing its excess energy in the form of light. This release of energy is called *spontaneous emission.*

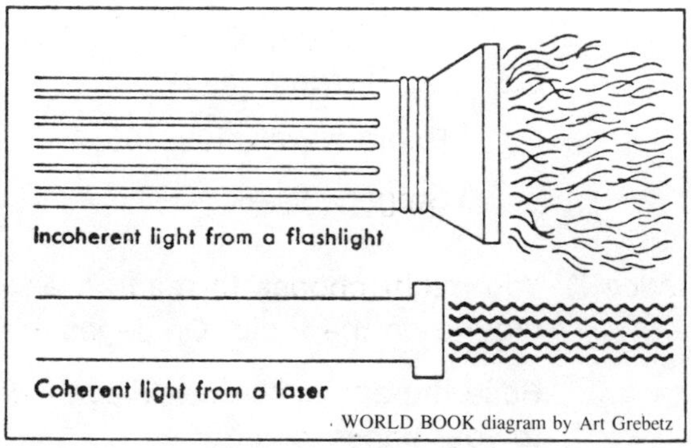

Lasers Produce Coherent Light. Waves of coherent light, unlike waves of incoherent light, move "in step" with one another. As a result, they spread only slightly — even over great distances.

In spontaneous emission, excited atoms release light irregularly. As a result, the light has different frequencies and travels in different directions. Light released in this way is called *incoherent light.* Such light is produced by the sun and by ordinary electric bulbs.

Excited atoms also may release light systematically. This kind of release, called *stimulated emission,* is the main process that takes place in a laser. Stimulated emission occurs when the energy released from one atom interacts with another atom that is still excited. The interaction triggers the excited atom into releasing its own extra energy as light. Most of the light produced by stimulated emission has the same frequency as the triggering light. It also travels in the same direction, and so it combines with and amplifies the triggering light. Such light is called *coherent light.*

The basic parts of a laser include a power source and a light-amplifying substance. Stimulated emission results when energy from the power source interacts with excited atoms in the substance. The total energy produced by a laser is always less than the energy produced by the power source. But the laser produces a much more intense light.

1. The rest of the article is concerned with kinds of lasers and the history of lasers. Would you want to read these sections for your paper?

   ____

2. On the lines below, list the different rates of reading that you used for this article. For each rate, list one example of a section in the article where you used that rate.

   RATE **SECTION**

   ____

   ____

   ____

   ____

Practice 8: Once you've read the relevant parts of the encyclopedia article, you have some basic information about lasers. At this point you may want to outline your paper, or you may choose to read further first.

Another source of information is journal articles. Read the relevant parts of the article on page 89. Be sure to *read flexibly.*

Place a check in the margin next to each paragraph which is relevant to your topic.

When you've finished reading, answer the questions on page 89.

SEEKING COHERENT ANSWERS

Laser Researchers Are Developing Coherent-light Solutions To A Host of Existing Challenges

by Janet Raloff

Every year more and more lasers are sent from the research community to be used in commerce and industry. They are already employed reading prices off products crossing supermarket checkout counters, welding detached retinas, cutting through steel and shooting three-dimensional movies. The next wave of recruits may enrich uranium, broadcast messages through the ocean to converse with submarines, or reduce the "noise" in audio and optical recordings. What follows is a glimpse of the diversity in research programs attempting to generate such recruits.

MEDICINE

Lasers entered the surgical theater during the late 1960s. Their ability to direct intense beams of energy into tissue without requiring either mechanical or electrical contact eliminated much of the trauma — such as tissue charring — associated with previous attempts to treat medical problems with heat.

So that neither a bleeding body nor a laser had to be tilted radically for a lesion or tumor to make proper contact with the scalpel-like beam, most early efforts in laser surgery focused on external tissues. But laser optics and advances in optical fibers — those flexible, hair-thin glass rods — have changed that. Carried inside endoscopes (medical instruments for viewing interior organs and canals), optical fibers now permit the intense and powerful beams of modern lasers to be curved and moved throughout the body's internal cavities without jarring a laser system's fragile and precisely aligned components. And certain sophisticated laser systems permit beam-exit ports to virtually dance over a patient's body at the surgeon's command. This resulting freedom has encouraged surgeons to explore internal use of laser cauterization and vaporization.

Richard Dwyer notes that lasers provide one of the safer ways to coagulate bleeding gastrointestinal ulcers. According to the University of California researcher at Harbor General Hospital in Torrance, "The success rate of the argon laser on selected patients is roughly 80 percent, and the success rate of the [neodymium: yttrium-aluminum-garnet laser] on unselected bleeding patients is 90 percent." What's more, endoscopic-laser surgery "can replace emergency surgery for . . . bleeding with elective surgery," Dwyer claims, adding that this procedure not only is safer for the patient, but also reduces the hospital stay required, blood transfusions necessary and days of work lost by the patient.

And for sleuthing tooth decay, lasers provide a simple and convenient tool to detect developing cavities, F. Sundstrom of the Karolinska Institute in Stockholm and H. Bjelkhagen of Sweden's Royal Institute of Technology reported at CLEO. Carious lesions in tooth enamel show up as dark spots when illuminated with blue light from an argon-ion laser. "Even initial pit and fissure lesions are clearly visible." And the procedure they developed makes it possible to spot these decay signs before they would otherwise be detectable with either visible light or ultraviolet fluorescence, they say.

DATA REPRODUCTION

Videodiscs promise to do for video what phonograph records did for sound — make prerecorded high-quality offerings available as affordable home entertainment. In commercial videodiscs today, images are recorded as a binary code spelled out in combinations of pits and spaces-without-pits. A tiny, focused laser beam burns these pits into a recording platter. To play back the images, a light passes over the disc. The presence or absence of pits triggers a photoelectric receptor to translate the encoded message into electrical signals which are eventually converted into a television picture.

1. What part(s) of the article did you skim?

____

____

2. What part(s) did you read in detail?

____

____

3. What part(s) did you omit?

____

____

UNIT IX SUMMARY: READING FLEXIBLY

Flexible reading means learning to vary your reading rate according to:

1. The kind of material you are reading
2. The purpose for which you are reading
3. The difficulty of the reading material for you

Think of flexible reading as shifting into different gears depending on what you are reading and for what purpose.

Four different reading rates are:

1. Skimming and scanning rate	Reading only key words, phrases, and sentences. Or, quickly searching for particular information. A very fast rate useful for surveying and finding specific information.
2. Rapid reading rate	Pushing your normal reading rate faster on purpose. Useful when you are reading only for main ideas or for review.
3. Average reading rate	The rate at which you ordinarily read material of average difficulty. Useful when you want to know details as well as main ideas.
4. Slow reading rate	Reading more slowly and deliberately than your average reading rate. Useful for difficult and/or technical reading.

For actual reading, you'll want to use several or all four rates while you read a chapter or article. The skilled reader changes gears often.

Reading flexibly can help you do research for research papers more effectively and efficiently. For example, you can skim or scan the entries in a card catalogue to find ones which are relevant for your topic. Once you locate useful books, you can skim their indexes to help you locate passages in the books which are directly related to your topic.

When you read any sources, for example, journal articles or articles in encyclopedias or elsewhere, you can use skimming, rapid reading, average reading, and slow reading as these rates are helpful to you.

LEARNING STUDY SKILLS ON YOUR OWN: IX

Speed Reading

Most people learn to read by saying single words aloud. When we take the next step and begin to read silently, we still "say" each word to ourselves in our thoughts. This is called *sub-vocalizing,* that is, "speaking" to ourselves without saying the words aloud.

Though we learn to read more complex and demanding material, most of us don't read any faster at 18 or at 48 than we did in sixth grade. Why? We continue to sub-vocalize as we read. Since we can only speak at most at about 180 words per minute, we can't read any faster than our sub-vocalizing allows.

Speed reading means learning to read without sub-vocalizing. The human mind is easily able to read without saying each word "aloud." Instead, we can learn to see words and understand them. When we learn to stop sub-vocalizing, we can increase our reading speed to 600 words per minute, 1000 words per minute, or even more. And with skilled speed reading, there is no loss of comprehension.

Of course, you can immediately see the value of speed reading in college. So how can you learn to speed read?

1. You can try to teach yourself. Work on breaking the habit of sub-vocalizing by trying to see groups of words and not saying them to yourself. If it's helpful, count as you read rather than say the words. Eventually you can let go of the counting as an aid.

   Also, teach yourself to use your hand (three fingers, two, one, or the whole hand) to underline each line of text as you read it. Move your hand lightly and quickly. Use your hand to help you move faster as you read and to keep yourself from going back over material again and again.

   Just by learning to stop sub-vocalizing and to use your hand to focus your attention and keep up your speed, you can easily *double* your effective reading rate.

2. If you need more instruction or help, find a self-taught speed reading course. One good text is *Speed Reading Made Easy* by Arlyne F. Rial (Garden City, NY: Doubleday, 1977). Or, take a speed reading course.

ISBN13: 9780810838550
90000
9780810838550

0-8108-3855-9
Scarecrow Press
1-800-462-6420
717-794-38000